Light and Sound

KT-379-774

Published in 2012 by Kingfisher
This edition published in 2013 by Kingfisher
an imprint of Macmillan Children's Books
a division of Macmillan Publishers Limited
20 New Wharf Road, London N1 9RR
Basingstoke and Oxford
Associated companies throughout the world
www.panmacmillan.com

ISBN 978-0-7534-3730-8

First published as *Kingfisher Young Knowledge: Light and Sound* in 2007
Additional material produced for Macmillan Children's Books by Discovery Books Ltd

Copyright © Macmillan Children's Books 2012

All rights reserved. No part of this publication may be reproduced, stored in or introduced
to a retrieval system or transmitted in any form or by any means (electronic, mechanical,
photocopying, recording or otherwise) without the prior permission of the publisher.
Any person who does any unauthorised act in relation to this publication
may be liable for criminal prosecution and civil claims for damages.

1 3 5 7 9 8 6 4 2
1SPL/0713/WKT/UTD/128MA

A CIP catalogue record for this book is available from the British Library.

Printed in China

Note to readers: the website addresses listed in this book are correct at the time of going to print.
However, due to the ever-changing nature of the internet, website addresses and content can
change. Websites can contain links that are unsuitable for children. The publisher cannot be held
responsible for changes in website addresses or content, or for information obtained through
a third party. We strongly advise that internet searches be supervised by an adult.

Acknowledgements
The publisher would like to thank the following for permission to reproduce their material. Every care has
been taken to trace copyright holders. However, if there have been unintentional omissions or failure to trace
copyright holders, we apologise and will, if informed, endeavour to make corrections in any future edition.
b = bottom, *c* = centre, *l* = left, *t* = top, *r* = right

Cover: Shutterstock/MarFot; Shutterstock/Elnur; Shutterstock/Kladej; Pages: 1 Alamy/Stockbyte; 2–3 Corbis;
4–5 Corbis/Zefa; 6–7 Getty/Stone; 7 Science Photo Library (SPL)/Larry Landolfi; 8*l* Corbis/Randy Farris; 9*tr* Getty/Stone;
9*bl* Natural History Picture Agency/James Carmichael Jr; 10–11 Alamy/Stock Connection; 12*c* Corbis/Walter Hodges;
12–13 Corbis/Zefa; 13*t* Nature Picture Library/David Shale; 14 Corbis; 15*t* Getty/Stone; 15*b* SPL; 16 Corbis/Aaron
Horowitz; 17*t* SPL/Celestial Image Co.; 17*b* Nature Picture Library/Jorma Luhta; 18–19 Corbis; 19*tl* Alamy/Phototake
Inc.; 20 Corbis/RoyMorsch; 21*t* Alamy/Imageshopstop; 21*b* SPL/Lawrence Lawry; 22 Getty/Photographer's Choice;
23*t* Alamy/Sami Sarkis; 23*b* SPL/NASA; 24 Brand X Pictures; 25*t* Corbis/NASA; 25*b* SPL/Custom Medical Stock Photo;
26 Alamy/Oote Boe; 27*t* SPL/Merlin Tuttle; 27 SPL; 28 Alamy/A T Willett; 28*t* Alamy/Imagestate; 30–31 Alamy/Butch
Martin; 31*c* Corbis/Zefa; 32*br* Getty/Imagebank; 32–33 Corbis/Zefa; 33*t* Getty/Imagebank; 34 Corbis/Bill Ross;
35*bl* Getty/Imagebank; 35*r* Corbis/Carmen Redondo; 36 Frank Lane Picture Agency/David Hosking; 37 Corbis;
37*br* Getty/Photodisc Red; 38 Getty/Johner Images; 39*tl* Alamy/Profimedia; 39*b* Getty/Photonica; 40*l* Photolibrary.com;
40*r* Corbis; 41*t* SPL/Hank Morgan; 41*b* SPL/NASA; 48*t* Shutterstock/xtrekx; 48*b* Shutterstock/Dhoxax; 49 NASA;
52 Shutterstock/HerrBullermann; 53*t* Wikimedia/NASA; 53*b* Wikimedia/Eric Rolph; 56 Shutterstock/Llike

Illustrations on pages: 8, 30 Sebastien Quigley (Linden Artists); 10, 11 Encompass Graphics

Commissioned photography on pages 42–47 by Andy Crawford
Thank you to models Mary Conquest, Darius Caple, Jamie Chang-Leng and Georgina Page

Light and Sound

Dr Mike Goldsmith

KINGFISHER

Contents

World of light   6

Eyes and seeing   8

Colour   10

Making light   12

Light from the Sun   14

Darkness and light   16

Shadows   18

Bouncing light   20

Bending light   22

Electric light   24

World of sound   26

What is sound?   28

How do we hear?   30

Making sound   32

34 How sound travels

36 Quiet or loud?

38 High or low?

40 Electric sound

42 Project: Shadow puppets

44 Project: Shadow clock

45 Project: Xylophone

46 Project: Plastic cup telephone

48 Glossary

50 Parent and teacher notes

52 Did you know?

54 Light and sound quiz

55 Find out more

56 Index

World of light

We need light to live. It gives us day and night, colours, pictures, stars and rainbows. We also use it to play CDs and to make electricity.

The bright Sun

The Sun is a star. It is a huge ball of burning gas that gives us light and warmth. Without it, there would not be any life on Earth.

Looking at the stars

Using telescopes, scientists can see more light from the stars. They can work out how far away from Earth they are, how hot they are and what they are made of.

Eyes and seeing

People need light to be able to see. Many night-time animals need less light to see than we do. They have big eyes, which take in as much light as possible.

retina

iris

pupil

lens

How people see
Light bounces off objects and into the eye through the pupil. The lens focuses the light on the retina and the brain works out what you are seeing.

Animal eyes

Night-time animals, like this owl, have huge eyes. They can see well in the dark and hunt at night.

eyes

Spider eyes

Spiders are hunters and need to catch insects to eat. Many spiders have eight eyes, so they can see in all directions at once.

Colour

People can see millions of different colours. Colours mix in different ways – all pigments mixed together make black, and all colours of light mixed together make white.

blue paint

yellow and blue mix to make green

red, yellow and blue mix to make black

red and blue mix to make purple

yellow paint

red and yellow mix to make orange

red paint

Mixing pigments

The colours of paints and dyes are made by mixing pigments. All colours other than red, yellow and blue can be made by mixing.

green light

red light

green and red mix to make yellow

all colours of light mixed together make white

blue and green mix to make cyan

blue light

red and blue mix to make magenta

Mixing lights

Lights mix in a different way to pigments. All colours are made by mixing different amounts of red, blue and green light.

Separating light

Sunlight (white light) is a mixture of colours. Raindrops separate these colours to make a rainbow of red, orange, yellow, green, blue, indigo and violet.

Making light

Anything will shine with light if it gets hot enough. Most of the light we see comes from hot objects, such as the Sun, light bulbs and stars.

Electric light

Some substances glow with light when electricity passes through them. When electricity is passed through neon gas, it gives out coloured light that can be used in advertising signs.

Living light

Some deep-sea fish make light from chemicals in their bodies. They use their light to catch food.

Birthday lights

Flames give off light as well as heat. The candles on this birthday cake glow brightly as they burn.

Light from the Sun

For billions of years, the Sun's light has shone on our world. It is millions of kilometres away, yet it is dangerous to look at it directly.

Life from light

Every living thing on Earth needs sunlight. The leaves of plants trap sunlight to grow.

Glowing sunsets

As the Earth turns, the Sun moves across the sky. When the Sun is low in the sky, it looks red because its light passes through the thick, dusty air near the ground.

Keeping warm

Heat from the Sun keeps the Earth's oceans liquid. Without it, all the water and air around the planet would be frozen.

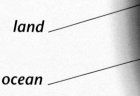

land

ocean

Darkness and light

When there is no light, we see darkness. Our planet spins in space – when it turns away from the Sun, it is night. We need other sources of light to see in the dark.

Moonlight

The Moon does not make its own light. Sunlight bounces off it and makes it glow.

Stars

Stars make their own light. Many are brighter than our star, the Sun. They look very faint because they are so far away.

Nature's light show

The Sun sends out particles that carry electricity. These can bounce off particles in the air, making the sky glow with different colours.

18 Shadows

When something blocks light, it casts a shadow. It is cooler and darker in the shadows because they are cut off from the Sun's warmth and light.

Shadows

All solid objects cast shadows. They may be long or short, depending on how the sunlight falls on them.

Darkness by day

Sometimes the Moon passes between the Earth and the Sun. It blocks our view of the Sun, causing darkness. This is called a solar eclipse.

Bouncing light

Light bounces off most objects. A lot of light bounces off snow, so it shines brightly in sunlight. Coal hardly lets any light bounce back from it, so it is dark.

Seeing double

The surface of a mirror is so smooth that it bounces back light in exactly the same pattern as it receives it. This is called a reflection.

Bright nights

In this picture, the Sun's light has bounced off the Moon to the sea, making the sea shine with light.

Talking with light

Light can travel through glass threads called optical fibres. These fibres can carry telephone calls and computer signals.

Bending light

Objects that light can travel through are called transparent. When light enters a transparent substance – such as glass or water – it bends.

Funny shapes
When light travels between water and air it bends, and what we see seems out of shape. The bending light has made this boy's body look bigger in the water.

Transparent life

Some sea creatures, such as this jellyfish, are transparent. It makes them very hard to see in the deep and murky waters.

Bigger and brighter

Magnifying lenses are fatter in the middle. They bend the light and make things look bigger than they are.

Electric light

Light can make electricity and electricity can make light. In a light bulb, electricity heats up a thin wire so that it glows.

Electric light
By colouring the glass of these light bulbs, different coloured lights are produced. Light bulbs get hot when switched on, so do not touch them.

Solar power
Solar panels outside this space station collect sunlight and turn it into electricity. The electricity is then used as power.

Laser surgery
Very narrow beams of light, called lasers, can be used for many things. They are used for delicate operations, such as eye surgery.

World of **sound**

There are sounds all around us. We listen to music and hear voices. Sound has many other uses, too. It can 'draw' pictures and help animals to find their prey.

Unwelcome sounds
Sounds that are unpleasant to listen to, such as the sound of heavy drills, are called noise.

Sounds in the dark

Bats use sound to hunt.
They give a shrill call
that bounces off any
solid object. They hear
the echo and work out
where their food is.

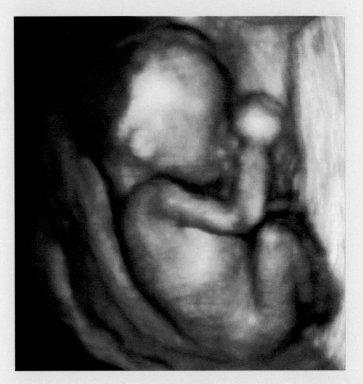

Sounds healthy

Doctors use sound
to create pictures of
unborn babies. Sound
waves bounce off the
baby, and computers
can 'draw' the picture.

(28) What is sound?

Sound is a sort of wave, or ripple. Like ripples in a pond, sound travels in all directions. The sounds get quieter the further you are from their source.

Boom!
Some planes travel faster than sound. They make a shock wave in the air. This can be heard as a loud bang, called a sonic boom.

Silent space

Sound can travel through air or water. There is no air or water in space so there is no sound.

Sound speeds

Sound travels quicker through water than through air. These orca use clicks and whistles to communicate underwater.

How do we hear?

When sound enters the ear, it travels down a tube. The tube's end is covered by a very thin wall of skin, called the eardrum.

tiny bones

ear tube or canal

nerve

eardrum

Inside the ear

When a sound hits the eardrum, it wobbles and makes the tiny bones inside the ear vibrate.

Hearing

Nerves in the ear send
messages to the brain.
The brain works out what
sound is being heard.

Animal ears

Most animals can hear, but
few have ears like ours. The
fennec fox has huge ears.
They can turn round to pick
up the slightest sound.

Making sound

Sound is usually made when something moves backwards and forwards very quickly. The moving thing might be a leaf in the breeze, the metal of a bell or a guitar string.

Musical sounds

Blowing a trumpet makes a buzzing sound in the mouthpiece. This sound travels through the trumpet to make music.

Voices

When you speak or sing, two flaps of skin in your throat wobble. These are called vocal cords.

Snaps and crackles

Sound can be a burst, like a balloon popping or fireworks exploding. We hear the crackles and fizzes while watching the lights.

How sound travels

Sounds travel as waves through air, water or solid objects. The waves eventually die away, but they can cover great distances first.

Long journeys
A busy street is a noisy place. The sounds of people talking, cars and other vehicles can travel a long way.

Echoes

Sound waves bounce back from hard objects, such as walls. We call these sounds echoes.

the echo bounces off the cave wall and the same shout is heard again

child shouts

Quiet or loud?

The more a sound wave wobbles, the louder it sounds. One of the loudest natural sounds is when a volcano erupts. Bombs and rocket engines make the loudest human sounds.

Shhh...

Some animals can hear sounds that are too quiet for people. An aardvark can hear termites crawling under the ground.

Ouch!

Very loud sounds can damage your ears. Our ears tense up when they hear loud noises, making everything sound muffled.

High or low?

Sound waves wobble at different speeds.
The faster the sound waves wobble,
the higher the sound they produce.
Sounds that wobble slower are lower.

Making music

Violin strings move
quickly and make a high
sound. Most guitar strings
move more slowly, so
their sound is lower.

High mews and low roars

Kittens have small vocal cords and weak lungs so they make high, quiet mews. Lions are big cats with powerful lungs. They make low, loud roars.

Electric sound

Sound can be changed into electricity. The electricity can then be changed back into sound again. This happens when you speak on the telephone.

Microphones

A microphone changes sound into a wobbling pattern of electricity. A loudspeaker turns these patterns back into sounds.

loudspeaker

microphone

Changing sound

By turning sounds into pictures like this one, scientists can see what we hear. These pictures are called sonograms.

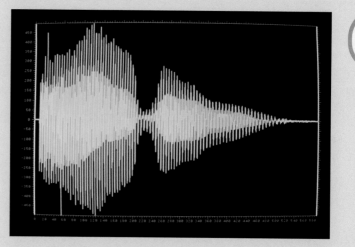

Voices from space

When astronauts are outside the spacecraft, they communicate using microphones and loudspeakers.

Shadow puppets

Make animal puppets

Solid shapes block the light and cast shadows. You can make different-shaped shadows, such as this dragon, and put on a shadow puppet show.

You will need
- Pencil
- Coloured paper
- Scissors
- Sweet wrappers
- Sticky tape
- Drinking straw or stick
- Torch

Draw a dragon with a long, pointed tail, feet and an open mouth on coloured paper.

Carefully cut out the dragon with scissors. Ask an adult to help with the tricky bits.

On one side, stick sweet wrappers to make flames coming out of the dragon's mouth.

You can make other shadow puppets, like a cat or a bird.

Tape a drinking straw or short stick to the back. Turn the dragon over and draw an eye, nose and wings.

In a darkened room, ask a friend to shine a torch on to a plain wall. This will make shadows.

Position your shadow puppet in front of the torch and move it around in the light.

Shadow clock

Tell the time by shadows

Shadow clocks measure time using shadows cast by the Sun. Have fun making your own clock.

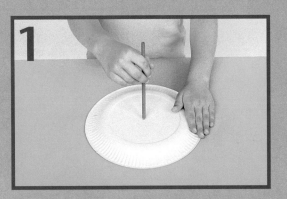

Make a small hole in the middle of a paper plate and stand a drinking straw upright in the hole.

You will need
- Paper plate
- Drinking straw
- Felt-tip pens

Keep your clock in the same place, and when the shadows fall, you'll be able to tell the time.

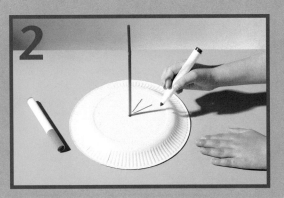

Put the plate in a sunlit place. Every hour, draw a line along the shadow the straw makes and note the time.

Xylophone

Make music

You can make a simple xylophone with glasses of water and a wooden spoon.

You will need
- 5 glasses, all the same size
- Jug of water
- Food colouring
- Wooden spoon

Line the glasses up and pour water into them. Fill the first right to the top, then the rest with a little less than the one before.

You can add a few drops of different food colourings to the glasses to colour the water.

Gently tap each glass with the spoon and you will hear that each one makes a different sound.

Plastic cup telephone

Make a working phone

You can make sound travel along a piece of stretched-out string. The plastic cups work as the microphone and the loudspeaker so that you can hear what your friend is saying.

You will need
- 2 plastic cups
- Stickers and coloured paper
- Scissors
- Modelling clay
- Sharp pencil
- Piece of string, 4–6 metres long

Decorate two clean, empty plastic cups with stickers and shapes cut from different coloured paper.

The sound of your voice travels along the string.

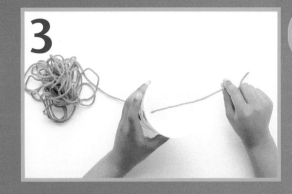

Place a ball of modelling clay under each cup and make a hole in the bottom with a sharp pencil.

Thread one end of the string through the hole, then tie a knot at the end.

Do the same with the other cup. Give a friend one cup and stretch out the string. Talk into the cup.

If your friend holds the other cup to his ear, he will hear what you are saying.

Glossary

Blocks – gets in the way of

Chemicals – substances used in chemistry

Communicate – to send a message to another creature

Damage – to hurt or cause injury

Delicate – easily broken or damaged

Echo – a sound that bounces off an object

Frozen – turned to ice

Gas – a shapeless substance, such as air, that is not solid or liquid

Iris – the coloured part of the eye

Liquid – a runny substance

Loudspeaker – a device that changes electricity into sound

Lungs – the parts inside the body that are used for breathing

Magnifying – making something seem bigger than it is

Mouthpiece – the part that goes over, or into, the mouth

Natural – occurring in nature, not made by people or machines

Neon – an invisible gas that glows when electricity passes through it

Nerves – special fibres that run from the brain to all parts of the body

Optical fibres – thin threads of glass along which light can pass

Particles – extremely small pieces

Pigments – substances that give something its colour

Prey – an animal that is hunted and killed by another animal

Produce – to make, or create

Produced – made

Reflection – the image you see when you look in a mirror, glass or very clear, still water

Retina – a special layer at the back of the eye that picks up light

Separating – splitting apart

Solar – to do with the Sun

Solar eclipse – when the Moon passes between the Earth and the Sun and causes darkness

Solar panel – a panel that collects sunlight and turns it into electricity

Sonic boom – the noise created when something travels faster than sound

Sonogram – a computer-generated picture of a sound

Source – where something comes from; for example, the Sun is a source of light

Telescope – an invention that makes things that are a long way away look closer

Transparent – see-through, or clear

Vehicles – machines used for transporting people or things

Vibrate – to move rapidly to and fro

Vocal cords – flaps of skin that enable humans to speak

This book includes material that would be particularly useful in helping to teach children aged 7–11 elements of the English and Science curricula, and some cross-curricular lessons involving History and Art.

Extension activities

Writing
Make a list of all the uses of light. Put them into alphabetical order. Add definitions and you have a dictionary of the uses of light!

Find all the times animals are mentioned in this book. Create a table with a picture of each one and facts about how they use light or sound.

Write a poem describing the sounds you hear through the day.

Imagine that someone made a machine to stop sunlight reaching the Earth. Write a newspaper report about what happened. Write a story about how the machine could be turned off.

Speaking and listening
Use this book to create a two-minute presentation entitled 'The top five things you need to know about light'.

Science
This book is about the topics of light and sound, but it also includes the themes of Earth and space (pp6–7, 14–15, 16–17, 19, 21, 25, 29, 41) and electricity (pp12, 24–25, 40–41).

Can you make up an experiment to find out if light and sound travel at the same speed? With a friend, get them to bang a metal pole with a big stick while you stand 20 metres away. Start a stop watch when you see them hit the pole, stop it when you hear the sound. Now think about measuring the speed of light with your friend holding a torch. What do your timings show?

Read the information about bats on page 27. Use the Internet or the library to find other animals that use echoes. How do humans use them?

Cross-curricular links

Art and design: Look at pages 10–11. Design a spinner with equal-sized sections coloured red, blue, green, yellow, orange and violet. Spin your spinner. What colour do you see? Why? Experiment with other colour combinations.
Look at the six colours on page 11. Which would you describe as warm colours and which are cold? Make a warm or a cold pattern picture using only those colours.

Make a collage of the Sun and Moon with moving parts so that you can show an eclipse.

History: Find the information on shadow clocks. Are there any shadow clocks (also known as sundials) on or near buildings in your area? Can you find out the history behind them?

Using the projects

Children can follow or adapt these projects at home. Here are some ideas for extending them:

Page 42: How can you make the shadow bigger or smaller? Use shadow to draw the outline of a friend's face onto a large piece of white paper or card.

Page 44: How would the lines be different if the clock was put on a sunny wall?

Page 45: What makes the sound low or high in pitch? Try bottles instead of glasses, and blow across the top of them. Can you make a stringed instrument with differently pitched notes?

Page 46: What happens if you don't keep the string tight? What happens if you coat the string with modelling clay? Can you find a way to make the sound louder? Can you find a way to bounce sound?

Did you know?

- One of the loudest sounds on record is the blue whale singing!

- Doctors use optical fibres to see inside patients' bodies.

- John Cage wrote a piece of music called *4 minutes and 33 seconds*. It is 4 minutes and 33 seconds of no music at all, so the audience can listen to the other sounds around them.

- There is no sound in space. Astronauts have to use radios in their helmets to communicate with each other.

- The body of a glow worm contains chemicals that make light!

- Dolphins and bats use sounds to make a 'picture' of their surroundings, so they can hunt for food.

- Before glass mirrors were invented, the Romans and Greeks used polished bronze to see their reflections.

- Lightning strikes the Earth around 100 times every second.

- The sperm whale uses powerful bursts of sound to stun and kill its prey!

- In a thunderstorm you can see lightning before you hear thunder. This is because light travels faster than sound.

- You can tell the time of day using shadows. Shadows are short in the middle of the day, when the Sun is high in the sky. In the early morning or late afternoon, the Sun is near the horizon and shadows are much longer.

- When you turn on an old-fashioned light bulb, only 10 per cent of the electricity used is changed into light. The rest is wasted as heat.

- Fish have ears inside their bodies. They make noises to find out where they are, to listen for enemies and even to find food!

- One of the loudest man-made sounds is that made by a rocket blasting off. Once it enters space, however, it is silent because there is no air.

- The smallest bone in your body is in your ear. It is called the stirrup bone and is only 3.3 millimetres long.

- On the Moon the sky is black, because there is no air to scatter the light.

- Some grasshoppers have ears on their legs!

- The speed of light is the fastest thing we know – it travels at about 300,000 kilometres per second. It takes light about 8 minutes to reach the Earth from the Sun.

- Sound travels around four times faster through water than it does through air.

- Rainbows form when sunlight shines through millions of raindrops.

Light and sound quiz

The answers to these questions can all be found by looking back through the book. See how many you get right. You can check your answers on page 56.

1) What colour is made if you mix red and blue?
   A – Green
   B – Orange
   C – Purple

2) If all colours of light are mixed together what colour do they make?
   A – Black
   B – White
   C – Cyan

3) Without heat from the Sun, the Earth's oceans would what?
   A – Stay as they are
   B – Freeze
   C – Change colour

4) Why is part of the Earth dark at night?
   A – It is facing away from the Sun
   B – The Moon blocks the Sun
   C – The Sun spins away from the Earth

5) What is it called when the Moon passes between the Earth and the Sun?
   A – A lunar eclipse
   B – A solar eclipse
   C – A star eclipse

6) What do optical fibres carry along them?
   A – Light
   B – Water
   C – Heat

7) What do magnifying lenses do?
   A – Bend light to make things look smaller
   B – Make things look the same
   C – Bend light to make things look bigger

8) What are the flaps of skin in your throat that wobble when you sing or speak called?
   A – Larynx
   B – Tonsils
   C – Vocal cords

9) How do sounds travel through the air?
   A – As waves
   B – As straight lines
   C – As long curved lines

10) Which is the loudest sound?
    A – A volcano erupting
    B – A wave breaking
    C – A child shouting

11) What is the brightest light on Earth?
    A – A firework
    B – A light bulb
    C – The Sun

12) What is the word given to the image you see when you look in a mirror?
    A – A refraction
    B – A reflection
    C – A shadow

Books to read

Hands-On Science: Sound and Light by
  Jack Challoner, Kingfisher, 2013
Light and Sound (Little Science Stars) by
  Clint Twist, Tick Tock Books, 2009
Light and Sound by John Clark, Red Kite
  Books, 2008
Super Science Experiments Light and Sound
  by Chris Oxlade, Miles Kelly Publishing
  Ltd, 2011

Places to visit

The Science Museum, London
www.sciencemuseum.org.uk
This amazing museum really brings the
world of science to life. With a fantastic
IMAX cinema, you can experience
stunning science films about the ocean,
space and much more in 3D.

The Australian Museum, Sydney
www.australianmuseum.net.au
Visit this museum and explore the
fascinating collections and exhibits it
has to offer. You can even take part in
a behind-the-scenes tour and visit areas
that are usually reserved for scientists!

Thinktank Museum of Science and
Discovery, Birmingham
www.thinktank.ac
Find out all about the world around
you at this exciting museum. You can
join crazy Coyote on an adventure
around the Earth, Moon and Sun
to discover eclipses, lunar phases
and much more.

Websites

*www.bbc.co.uk/schools/ks2bitesize/science/
physical_processes/light/play.shtml*
This fun game uses your knowledge of
light. Help Rani escape from Odd Bob
in the hall of mirrors.

*www.bbc.co.uk/schools/ks2bitesize/science/
physical_processes/shadows/play.shtml*
This game explores the topic of
shadows. Help Steve take a picture
of the king cobra, but make sure you
avoid the shadows!

www.learner.org/teacherslab/science/light/
Find information, games and
experiments all on the subject
of light on this fun website.

*www.fi.edu/fellows/fellow2/apr99/
soundindex.html*
This website contains lots of good
information and diagrams, all on
the subject of sound.

www.engineeringinteract.org
This website contains games based on
the science of light and sound. Help to
save the Earth from destruction using
the science of light in 'Alien Attack!' and
solve the fishy goings-on with the science
of sound in 'Ocean Odyssey!'.

*www.nasa.gov/audience/forstudents/
k-4/dictionary/Sound.html*
Learn about sound and find some
interesting activities to experiment with
sound on this NASA website.

animals 8, 9, 27, 29, 31, 36, 39, 52, 53
bending light 22–23
brain 8, 31
candles 13
colours 10–11
darkness 16–17
ears 30–31, 37, 53
echoes 27, 35, 52
electricity 6, 12, 24–25, 40–41
eyes 8–9
fish 13, 53
hearing 30–31, 52
lasers 25
loudspeakers 40, 41
magnifying lenses 23
microphones 40, 41
mirrors 20, 52
Moon 16, 19, 21, 53

music 26, 32, 38, 45, 52
night 16
noise 26
optical fibres 21, 52
rainbows 6, 11, 53
reflections 20, 52
shadows 18–19, 42–43, 44, 52
solar power 25
sonic boom 28
sonograms 27, 41
sound waves 27, 28, 34–35, 36, 38
stars 6, 7, 12, 17
Sun 6, 11, 12, 14–15, 16, 17, 18–19, 21, 44
telephones 40, 46–47
telescopes 7
transparent objects 22–23
voices 26, 33
water 22–23, 29, 45, 53

Light and sound quiz answers

1) C	7) C
2) B	8) C
3) B	9) A
4) A	10) A
5) B	11) C
6) A	12) B